Career Exploration
A Workbook Exploring STEM Careers

by Edward W. Smith

ISBN 13:978-1533124487   ISBN 10:1533124485

Instructions

This is a **Career Exploration Workbook About STEM Careers** by _____. Color the titles, pictures, education levels, and incomes. The author decides how the coloring is done. Occasionally coloring instructions will be given.

Helpers can decide when and how to explain the terminology and incomes. Incomes are U.S. median salaries. Median means middle, half earn more and half earn less. Occasionally you will see a + after the incomes.   These occupations earn more than the incomes shown.

Exploring careers is fun. Suggestions for good times to do the **Workbook.**

Today, we will have rain, snow, sleet, hail, and lots of wind. It is a very good day to **explore careers.**

STEM

Find the words in the grid. Words can go across and down only.

```
M A T H E M A T I C S
T V N G B R M V M S E
L R M Q J W R W Q C N
B F X G R B W M X I G
H M C J B M T C T E I
K N W N M S T E M N N
Y Z T R X L N Y Z C E
N X W N K T B D B E R
N Y D R C F K T F W I
T E C H N O L O G Y N
Q X C Z D H Z L T Q G
```

STEM
Science
Technology
Engineering
Mathematics

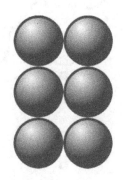

Money, Math & Jobs

Many jobs require you to work with money. Count the money and write the amount on the line.
Very few jobs do not require good math skills.

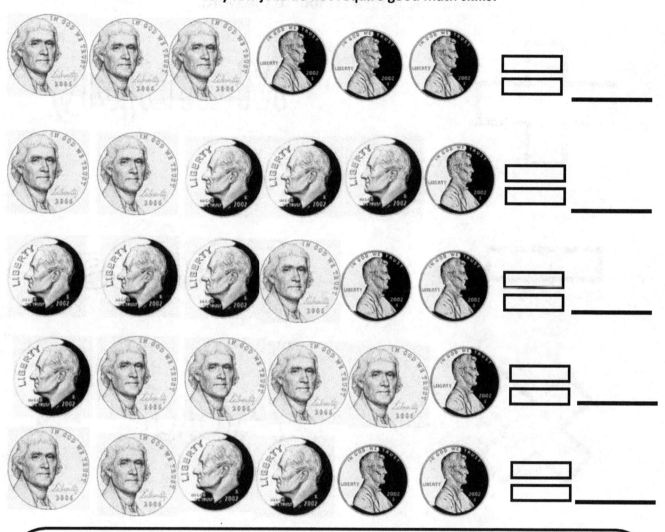

Draw or write about a person working at a job that requires good math skills.

Math Symbols

Draw a line from a symbol to the word.

 Multiply

 Equals

 Add

 Subtract

 Divide

Veterinarian

I help people keep their pets healthy.

College $85,000

Race Car Mechanic

I make sure race cars run properly and are safe.

High School + $60,000

Aircraft Mechanic

I inspect and maintain aircraft to make sure they are safe to fly.

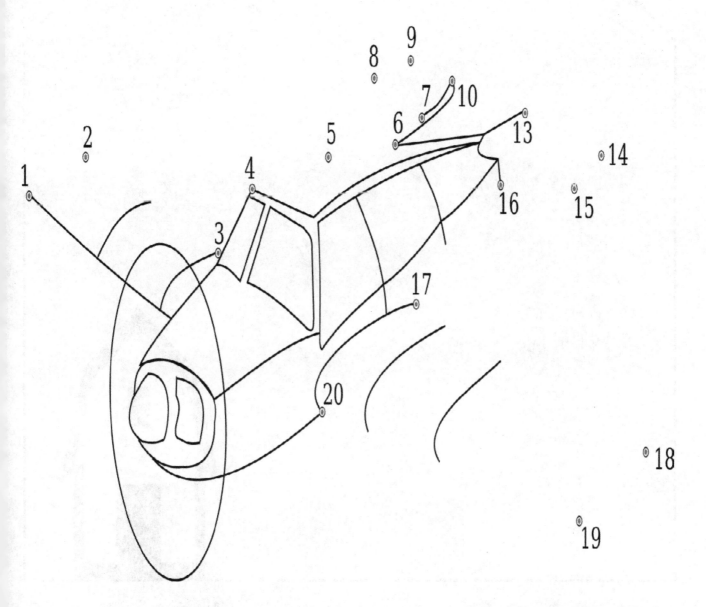

High School + 1 $56,990

Farmer

**I grow crops and animals for you to eat.
Draw fields with crops and animals I could grow.**

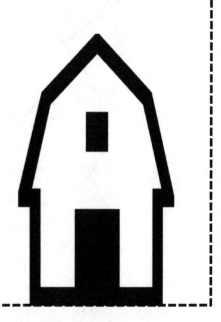

High School + $68,050

Teacher

I help kids learn what they want to do when they go to work.

College $50,000

Attorney

I defend people accused of crimes.

College $90,000

Meteorologist

I inform you about weather conditions.

College $75,000

Realtor

I sell residential houses.

High School + $41,000

Astronaut

I ride in the space shuttle and explore outer space.

College $140,000

Airline Pilot

I fly people safely to their destinations.

College $118,140

Helicopter Pilot

I fly a helicopter that catches rockets returning from outer space.

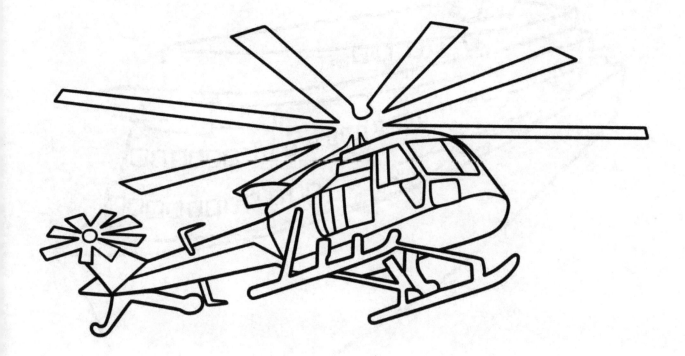

College $75,000

Ship Captain

I safely deliver passengers or cargo all over the world.

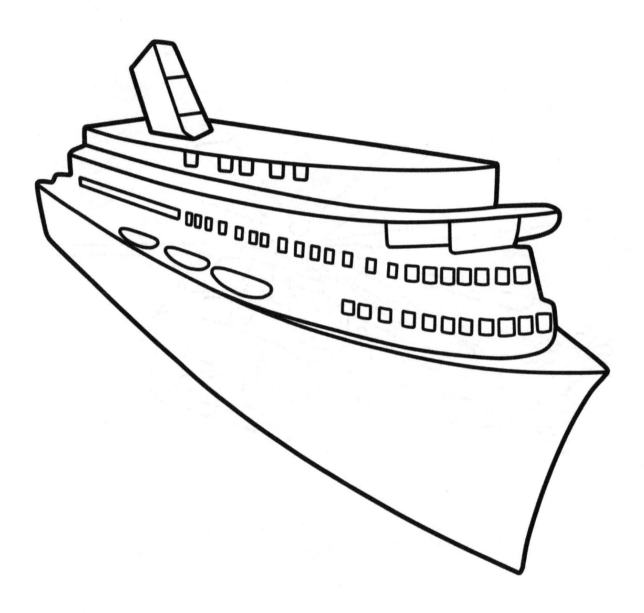

College $153,370

Dentist

I keep your teeth and gums healthy.

College $149,540

Medical Equipment Repairer

I test, adjust, or repair medical equipment.

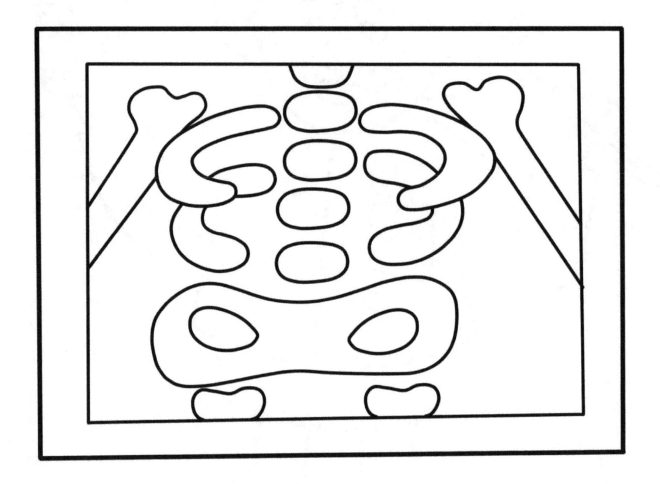

Education N.A. $45,660

Pharmacist

I get you the medicine your doctor prescribes for you.

College $121,000

Heavy Equipment Repair Instructor

I teach college students how to repair heavy equipment.

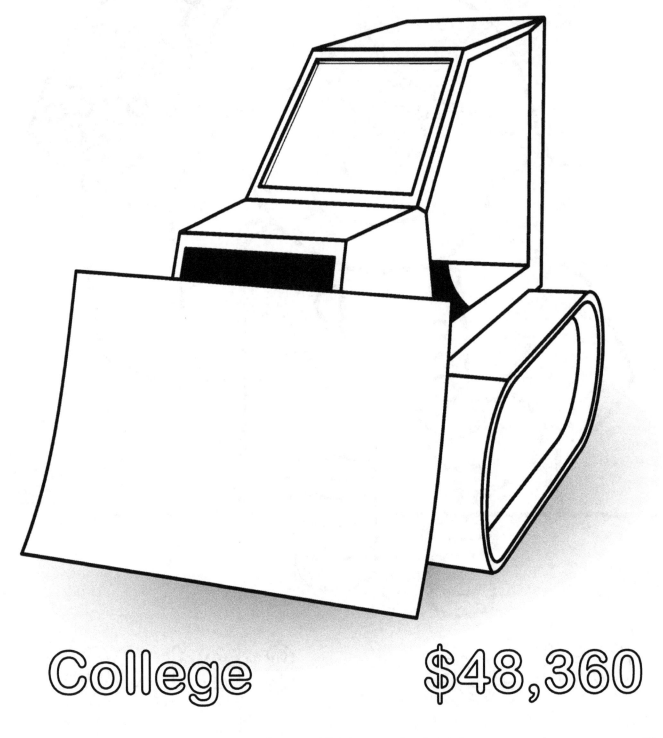

College $48,360

Crane Operator

I operate heavy lifting equipment.

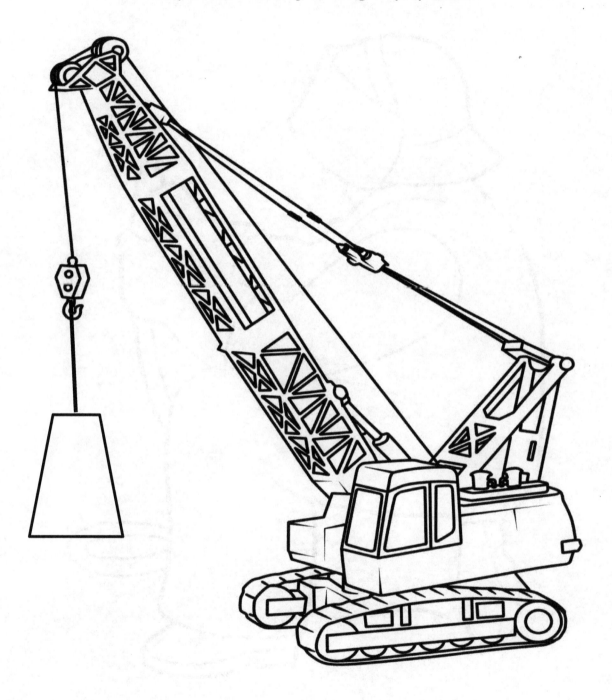

High School + 1 $50,720

Welder

I repair broken construction equipment.

High School + 1 $37,420

Electrician

I maintain and repair electric signs.

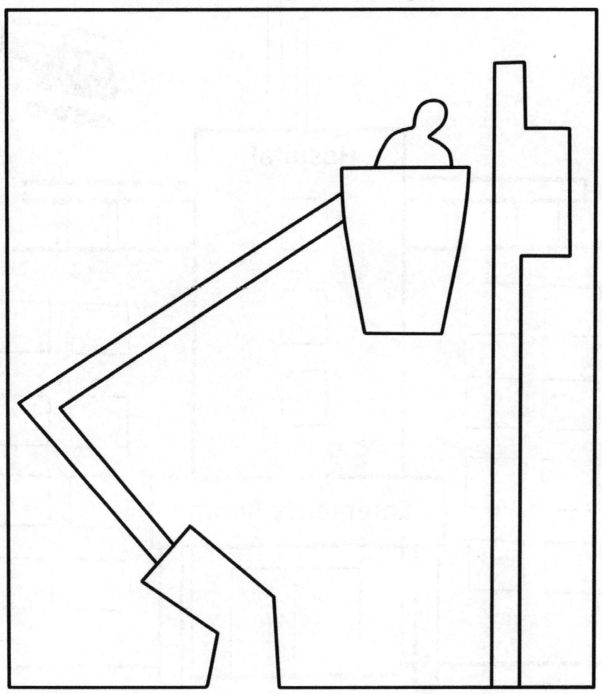

High School + 1-2 $51,000

Emergency Room Doctor

I provide care for sick or injured patients when they arrive at the hospital.

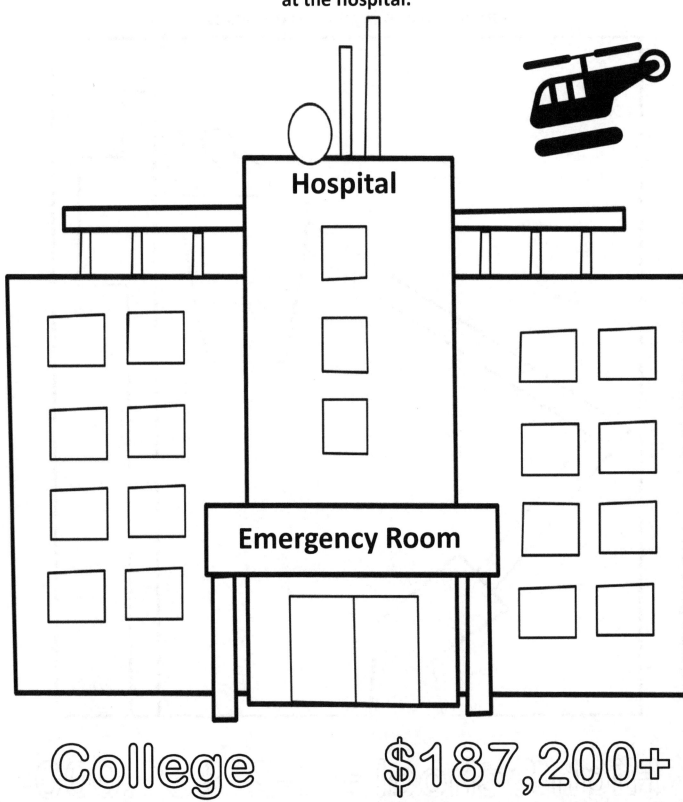

College $187,200+

STEM Occupations

Find the words in the grid. Words can go across and down only.

```
L W Q N J B R A N C H E R R C
H N W H N U R S E K N C K R A
P S C I E N T I S T J T T C P
H P Y D Z A R C H I T E C T T
A D T G H T T M B Q A D L A
R E R M E C H A N I C C O F I
M N B I O L O G I S T H C A N
A T K L M C L F L Z T E T R D
C I P R O G R A M M E R O M R
I S I S U R V E Y O R K R E A
S T L W B W K N N V H K T R F
T T O L J Q M F C H E M I S T
Y R T K D I E T I C I A N H E
P V E T E R I N A R I A N V R
C A R P E N T E R M C T K G M
```

Architect-$72,200	Dentist-$149,500	Mechanic-$37,120	Rancher-$68,050
Biologist-$58,270	Dietician-$56,950	Nurse-$66,640	Scientist-$69,110
Captain-$153,37	Doctor-$187,200	Pharmacist-$121,000	Surveyor-$57,050
Carpenter-$50,000	Drafter-$49,990	Pilot-$118,140	Teacher-$50,000
Chemist-$122,800	Farmer-$68,059	Programmer-$77,550	Veterinarian-$85,000

Paramedic/EMT

I provide emergency care and transport injured or sick people to the hospital.

High School + 2 $31,700

U.S. Navy

I help protect freedom of the seas.

High School + Math & Science

Computer Technician

I install and repair computers.

High School + 1-2 $47,610

Physical Therapist

I help patients improve or correct their physical disability.

College $82,390

College Professor

I teach math to college students.

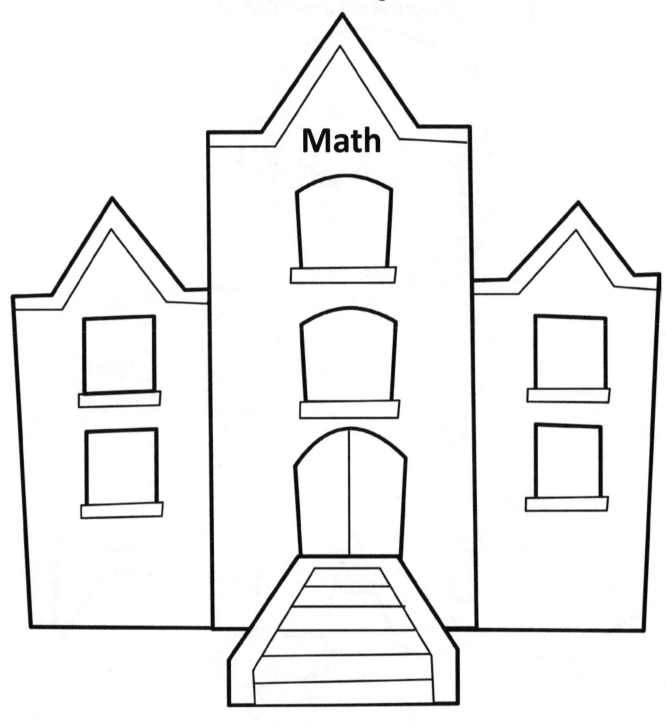

Math

Color title, education, income, and building using the school colors of a college in your area.

College

$65,190

Geologist

I study landforms and physical features.

College $89,910

Forester

I help maintain healthy forests and protect them from fire.

College $57,100

Wildland Firefighter

I control and put out fires.

High School +   # $45,500

Park Ranger

I conduct educational programs for park visitors.

NATIONAL PARK

College $61,860

Astronomer

I study planets, stars, and galaxies.

College $105,410

Wildlife Biologist

I study wildlife in their natural environment.

College $58,270

Architect

I design zoo exhibits.

College $74,520

Lab Technician

I help other scientists in the lab.

High School + 2 $44,180

Business Owner

I sell the products that my company makes.

College   Income N.A.

U.S. Army

I protect Americans from foreign aggression.

High School + Math & Science

Firefighter

I protect life and property and provide rescue efforts.

High School + 1 $45,600

Nurse

I provide care for patients in the hospital.

College $66,640

Computer Programmer

I write computer programs.

College $77,550

Traffic Enforcement Officer

I enforce traffic and pedestrian laws of the city.

High School + 1-2 $56,130

K-9 Officer

My partner and I patrol the streets and enforce the laws of the city.

High School + 1-2 $56,130

Nursery Manager

I sell plants, trees, and gardening supplies.

College $68,050

Wind Turbine Technician

I inspect and repair wind turbines.

College $48,800

STEM Occupations

Find the words in the grid. Words can go across and down only.
Two word occupations run together . Words in (   ) are not in the word search.

```
C W V C V A U D I T O R L K M D S T
R A M T M E D I C A L P A E O V O R
I T B L M P R O J E C T N Q R N I A
M E D R O N E P I L O T I U T V L N
E R R C K K N A C B K K M I H H S S
S R N K V M R R Y A W G A P O Y C P
C E L Q Y M R K B N R J L M D P I O
E S A P P S L R E K J K S E O G E R
N O C N J T L A R E J B C N N Y N T
E U C R B K F N S R T P I T T W T A
N R V T H D W G E L K L E F I R I T
W C P C L K N E C Q M D N T S R S I
P E J Y K T F R U B F B T T T Z T O
K Y Q R T D X G R J K R I C J B K N
R H K G R A P H I C D E S I G N E R
K Y K T T D M P T X M Z T M T N M V
L X Q N D M H H Y J B J C O O K L W
M O L E C U L A R V H W N N F V Y G
```

Apps (Designer)-$64,937

Animal (Scientist)-$61,110

Auditor-$65,940

Banker-$115,340

Cook-$$23,400

Cybersecurity (Analyst)-$70,475

Drone Pilot-N.A.

Crime Scent (Investigator)-$39,466

Electronics (Engineering Technician-$59,820

Forestry (Technician)-$35,260

Graphic Designer-$45,900

Equipment (Mechanic)-$31,800

Molecular (Biologist)-$74,720

Orthodontist-$187,200

Medical (Sonographer)-$67,500

Park Ranger-$61,860

Soil Scientist-$59,920

Transportation (Planner)-$76,330

Water (Resource Specialist)-$120,050

Construction Manager

I schedule and coordinate the work on construction projects.

College

$85,630

Exploring STEM Careers
Grades 1-3

Activity:

Begin the journey of your lifetime exploring exciting careers. This activity will help you match things you like with jobs you might like when you grow up. Begin by thinking about things you like to do.

Step 1: For this hands-on activity, you will need green, yellow, and red colored pencils. Color, following the rules for a stop light.

You like the activity, go ahead, & color the picture GREEN.

You are UNSURE, use caution, & color the picture YELLOW.

You DISLIKE the activity, stop, and color the picture RED.

Step 2: Count how many green_____, yellow_____, and red _____pictures you have.

Step 3: The green pictures are jobs you might like to do. The yellow pictures are probably activities you haven't done, or done often enough to know whether or not you like them. Put a question mark next to the yellow pictures. Red pictures are those activities you don't like at all. Cross the red pictures out!!

Step 4: Look back at the jobs that go with green pictures, and pick three. Remember, this activity is designed to help you explore a lot of careers! You might try this activity again in a month and see if your answers have changed.

On _____(Today's Date) I would most like to explore these jobs:

_____   _____   _____

Color your interests. Below are pictures of job activities. You will need green, yellow, and red crayons or colored pencils to color the stoplight next to your choices. Follow the same rules as the stop sign: green to go ahead to activities you like. Yellow for activities you are not sure about, and red for activities you don't like.

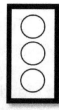

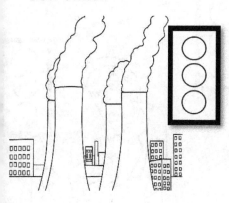

Manage power plant

Operate on patients

Sell products

Report the news

Take care of patients

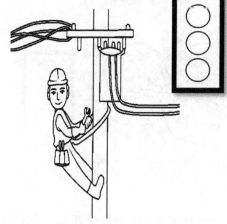

Repair electrical problems

Prepare meals

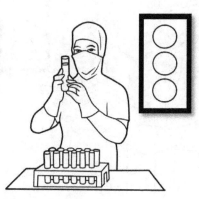

Work in a lab

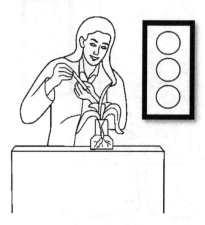

Study plants

Color your interests. Below are pictures of job activities. You will need green, yellow, and red crayons or colored pencils to color the stoplight next to your choices. Follow the same rules as the stop sign: green to go ahead to activities you like. Yellow for activities you are not sure about; and red for activities you don't like.

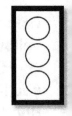

P.E. Teacher/Coach

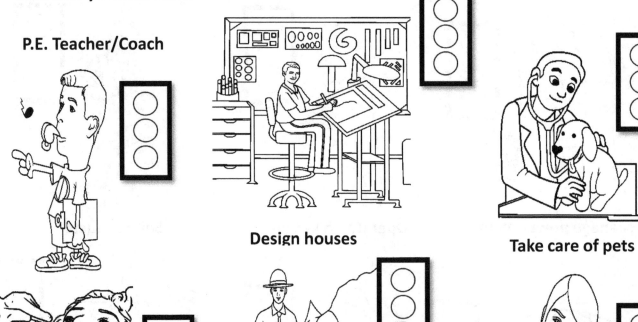

Design houses

Take care of pets

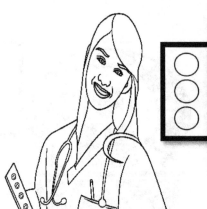

Keep your teeth clean **Enforce hunting & fishing regulations** **Keep people healthy**

Help doctors

Design office buildings

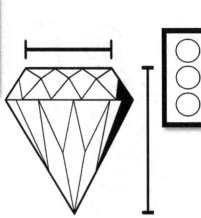

Sell expensive jewelry

Additional Career Exploration Work Books Available

Career Exploration Work Book About Careers – Grades 1-3

Career Exploration Work Book About Careers That Have:
    Rapid Growth
    Numerous Job Openings
    New & Emerging Occupations
                          Grades 4 - 6
Career Exploration Work Book About STEM Careers – Grades 5 – 9

Exploring Education & Training Options – Grades 8-10

Individual Career Exploration Work Books available at Amazon.com
Quantity prices available for schools, fund raisers, PTO 's, Scouts, Church Groups,
Boys & Girls Clubs, Big Brothers & Big Sisters, charitable donations, libraries, corp. id

For further information contact:
careeractivities@gmail.com

CPSIA information can be obtained
at www.ICGtesting.com
Printed in the USA
LVHW100708130720
660510LV00007B/126